Causes of the Civil War

A House Divided

Heather E. Schwartz

Consultants

Vanessa Ann Gunther, Ph.D.
Department of History
Chapman University

Nicholas Baker, Ed.D.
Supervisor of Curriculum and Instruction
Colonial School District, DE

Katie Blomquist, Ed.S.
Fairfax County Public Schools

Publishing Credits

Rachelle Cracchiolo, M.S.Ed., *Publisher*
Conni Medina, M.A.Ed., *Managing Editor*
Emily R. Smith, M.A.Ed., *Series Developer*
Diana Kenney, M.A.Ed., NBCT, *Content Director*
Courtney Patterson, *Senior Graphic Designer*
Torrey Maloof, *Editor*

Image Credits: Cover and pp. 1, 2, 9 (bottom right), 10, 11 (top), 12, 15 (bottom), 20, 26 North Wind Picture Archives; pp. 4-5, 13 (top and bottom), 18-19, 29 Granger, NYC; pp. 7 (top), 23 (bottom) Sarin Images/Granger, NYC; pp. 5 (top), 28 (left) LOC [LC-USZ62-79305]; p. 5 (bottom) Wikimedia Commons/ Public Domain; p. 6 DeAgostini/Getty Images; p. 7 (bottom) NARA [1667751]; pp. 11 (bottom), 21, 32 akg-images/ Newscom; p. 14 Al Fenn/The LIFE Picture Collection/Getty Images; p. 15 (top) NARA [301673], (middle) Public Domain; p. 16 (back) Walter Sanders/The LIFE Images Collection/Getty Images, (front) LOC [LC-DIG-ppmsca-31540]; p. 17 (front) Everett Collection/Newscom, (back) LOC [LC-USZ62-132561]; p. 18 (front) Pictorial Press Ltd/Alamy Stock Photo; p. 19 (top left) LOC [LC-DIG-cwpbh-05089], (top right) LOC [LC-USZ62-7816]; p. 23 (top) LOC [LC-USZC2-331]; p. 24 Bob Thomas/Popperfoto/Getty Images; p. 27 (bottom) LOC [LC-USZ62-5067], (top) LOC [LC-USZC2-2663]; p. 28 (right) LOC [LC-DIG-ppmsca-31540]; p. 31 Bob Thomas/Popperfoto/Getty Images; all other images from iStock and/or Shutterstock.

Library of Congress Cataloging-in-Publication Data

Names: Schwartz, Heather E., author.
Title: Causes of the Civil War : a house divided / Heather E. Schwartz.
Description: Huntington Beach, CA : Teacher Created Materials, Inc., 2017. |
Includes index.
Identifiers: LCCN 2016034158 (print) | LCCN 2016040662 (ebook) | ISBN
9781493838035 (pbk.) | ISBN 9781480757684 (eBook)
Subjects: LCSH: United States--History--Civil War,
1861-1865--Causes--Juvenile literature. | Slavery--Southern
States--History--Juvenile literature. | United States--Politics and
government--1849-1861--Juvenile literature.
Classification: LCC E459 .S25 2017 (print) | LCC E459 (ebook) | DDC
973.7/11--dc23
LC record available at https://lccn.loc.gov/2016034158

Teacher Created Materials
5301 Oceanus Drive
Huntington Beach, CA 92649-1030
http://www.tcmpub.com

ISBN 978-1-4938-3803-5

Printed by: 590835
Printed in: China

Table of Contents

One Step Toward War

"Once free, always free." This was a **doctrine** in the Missouri court system in the 1800s. In 1846, a slave named Dred Scott tested this policy. When his master died, he **sued** his master's wife for his freedom. Scott believed that since he had lived with his master in free territories, he should be a free man. The case went all the way to the U.S. Supreme Court. The Court's decision changed the course of history. It further divided a nation and pushed the country one step closer to war.

The years leading up to the Civil War were turbulent and tense. People were divided over **controversial** issues facing the country. The biggest issue was slavery. Many people wanted it to end. Others wanted to stop it from spreading. Some felt slavery was necessary. It was a hot topic. And it was one that would tear the nation apart.

The Supreme Court hears the Dred Scott case.

FRANK LESLIE'S
ILLUSTRATED
NEWSPAPER

NEW YORK, SATURDAY, JUNE 27, 1857.

This 1857 newspaper features an article about Dred Scott.

Dred Scott

A Delicate Balance

In the early 1800s, **debates** raged over slavery. There were also disagreements about states' rights. The nation was slowly splitting in two. A line was being drawn between the North and the South. Many Northerners were against slavery. They thought it should be banned in every state, not just the North. They felt the **federal** government should step in to **abolish** it. They did not think each state should have the power to permit slavery.

DIFFERENT LIVES

Some Southerners had large farms called *plantations*. They forced enslaved Africans to work on plantations without pay. They had no rights. The North had factories in cities. Workers were paid wages.

The U.S. debate on slavery was closely watched by other countries, as evidenced by this 1856 cartoon from British magazine, *Punch*.

The South felt the exact opposite. Southerners thought each state should be free to make its own laws. They did not want the federal government to interfere. The South thought slavery was a vital part of its **economy**. Southerners thought they would not be able to make enough money from their farms if they had to pay people to work the land.

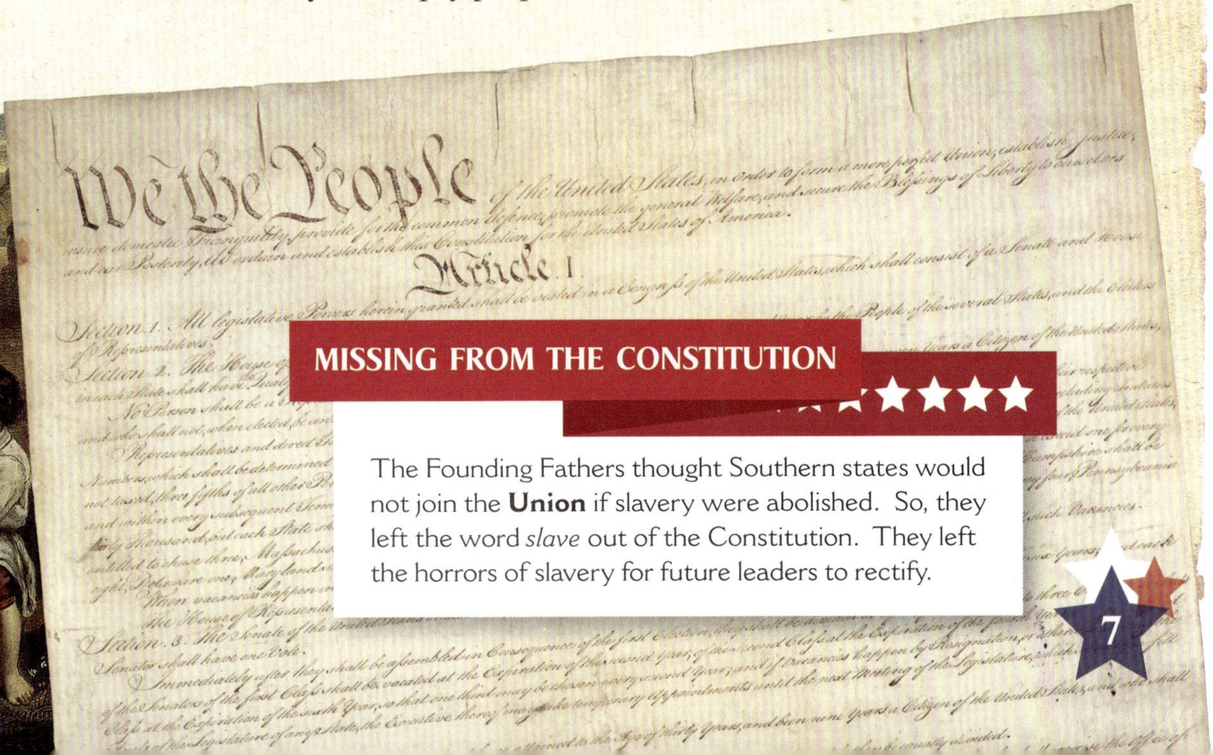

MISSING FROM THE CONSTITUTION

The Founding Fathers thought Southern states would not join the **Union** if slavery were abolished. So, they left the word *slave* out of the Constitution. They left the horrors of slavery for future leaders to rectify.

Missouri Compromise

During the 1800s, the United States was still growing. New territories joined the Union. Leaders had to make big decisions. Should slavery be allowed in the new states? Or should it be illegal? Leaders wanted to make both sides happy. So, they tried to strike a balance.

In 1819, the United States was made up of 22 states. There were 11 free states and 11 slave states. But Missouri also wanted to join the Union. This created a problem. Should Missouri be a free state or a slave state? The North and the South argued. Each state was represented in the federal government. Adding one more state to either side would give that side more power. It would have more votes in Congress. The dispute lasted two years.

Missouri Compromise

STILL NOT HAPPY

The Missouri Compromise did not unite the two sides. The North was angry that slavery spread into new territories. The South didn't like that the federal government was intervening.

In 1819, Maine applied to join the Union, too. This gave leaders an idea. Missouri would be a slave state. Maine would be a free state. The country would remain balanced. This solution was called the Missouri **Compromise**. The compromise also stated that all western territories above Missouri's southern border were free. All territories below it would allow slavery.

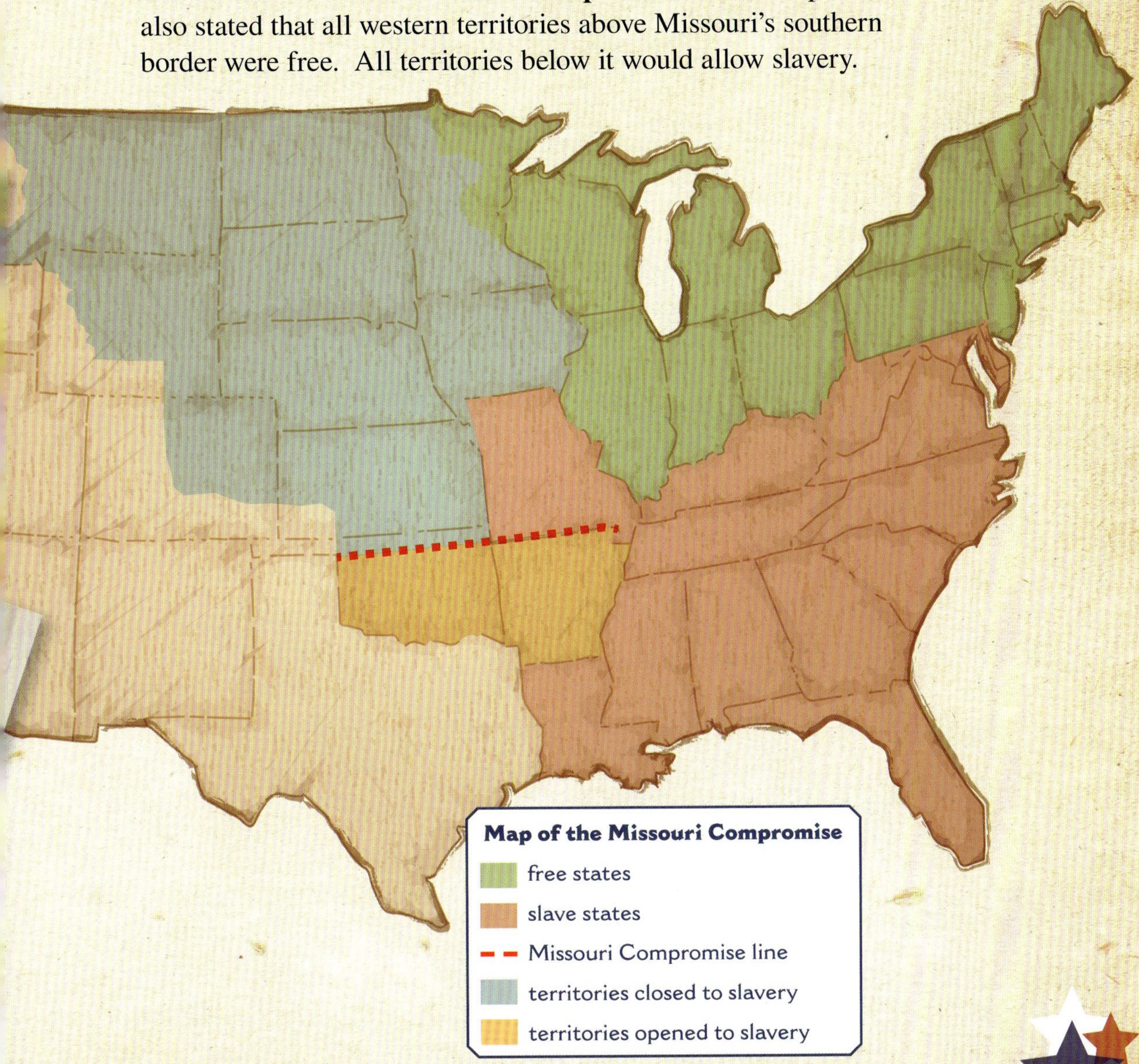

Compromise of 1850

In 1849, California sought to join the Union, and it didn't want slavery. Now, there would be more free states. Conflict between the North and South flared up as the balance between free states and slave states was upset once again. This led to a second compromise.

The Compromise of 1850 was an attempt to keep the peace. It stated that California would enter the Union as a free state. But the people living in New Mexico and Utah Territories would get to choose whether they wanted to be a free state or a slave state.

The Compromise also changed the Fugitive Slave Act and banned slave trading in Washington, DC. Slavery itself was still allowed. But, people could no longer be bought or sold there. This was a big deal. The largest slave market in the country was in DC. More slaves were traded there than anywhere else.

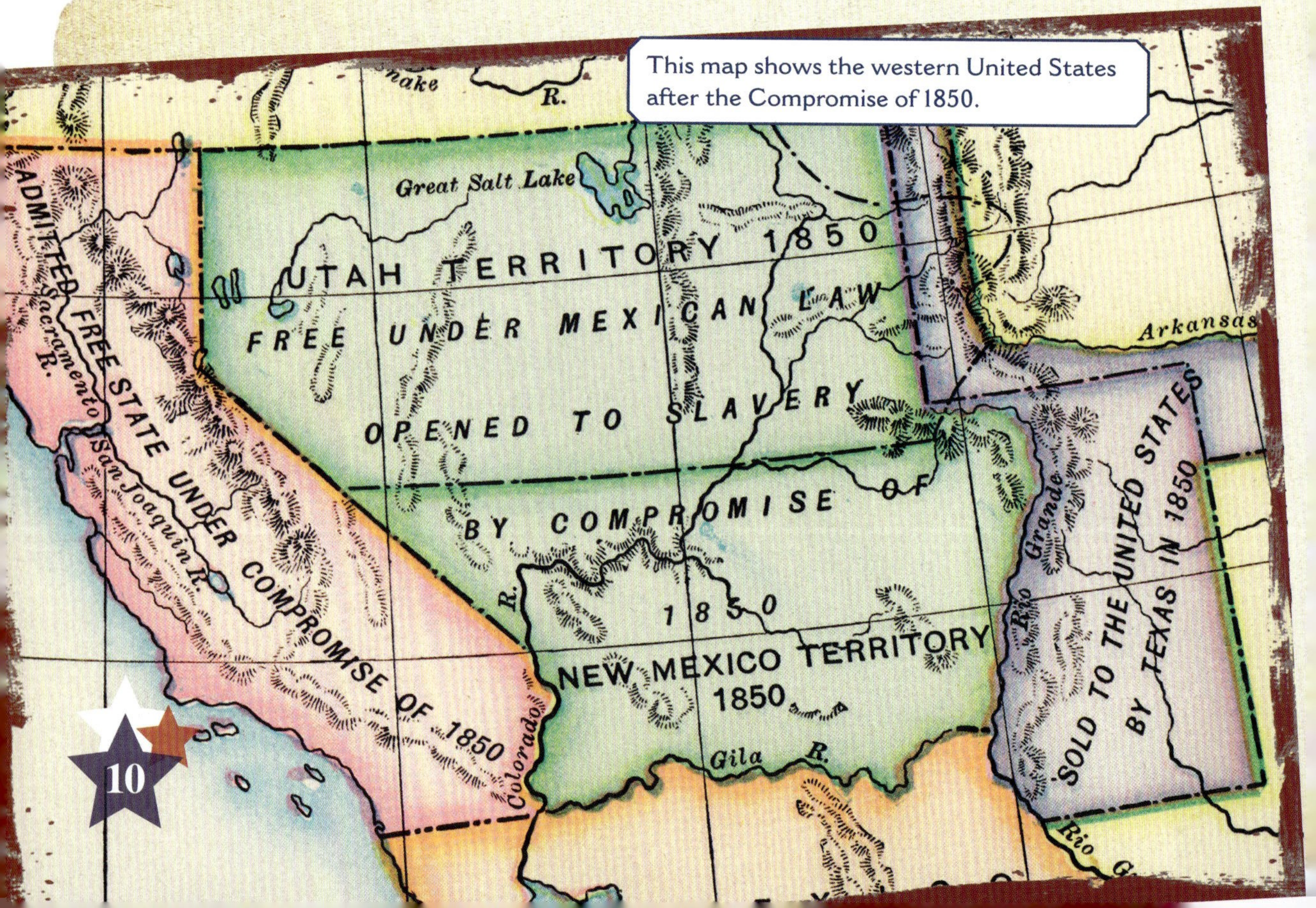

This map shows the western United States after the Compromise of 1850.

Two men capture escaped slaves under the Fugitive Slave Act.

FUGITIVE SLAVE ACT

Many people fled to the North to escape slavery. The Fugitive Slave Act allowed people to search for escaped slaves in the North. But in 1850, Congress changed the law. It said that Northerners must help return runaway slaves to their owners. It also set harsher punishments for helping people escape slavery. This upset many Northerners.

CAUTION!!

COLORED PEOPLE OF BOSTON, ONE & ALL,

You are hereby respectfully CAUTIONED and advised, to avoid conversing with the Watchmen and Police Officers of Boston,

For since the recent ORDER OF THE MAYOR & ALDERMEN, they are empowered to act as

KIDNAPPERS AND Slave Catchers,

And they have already been actually employed in KIDNAPPING, CATCHING, AND KEEPING SLAVES. Therefore, if you value your LIBERTY, and the *Welfare of the Fugitives* among you, *Shun* them in every possible manner, as so many *HOUNDS* on the track of the most unfortunate of your race.

Keep a Sharp Look Out for KIDNAPPERS, and have TOP EYE open.

APRIL 24, 1851.

Bleeding Kansas

In 1854, two more territories were ready to join the Union. Kansas and Nebraska now had enough people to become states. So, Congress passed the Kansas-Nebraska Act. This law allowed people in those territories to choose whether they wanted to be a free state or a slave state. This was very controversial. It reversed the Missouri Compromise. Both of these new states would have been free states. That is what was agreed to in the old compromise. People in the North were furious.

This antislavery symbol was called Liberty for Kansas.

Nebraska voted to be a free state. Many of the people living there were from the North. But, Kansas was closer to slave territory. It was unclear which way people would vote. People from other states, both in the North and in the South, flooded into Kansas. They wanted to influence voters. Some of them voted illegally. After the vote, it was declared that Kansas would be a slave state. Northerners were outraged. Fights broke out. Small battles were waged, and people died. The territory became known as "Bleeding Kansas."

This map shows how the Kansas and Nebraska territories were above the Missouri Compromise line.

People from Missouri vote for slavery in Kansas.

Big Decision

Before the Civil War, some people were thought of as property. They had no rights. Often, slave owners would take these enslaved people with them when they traveled or moved—even if they moved into a free state in the North.

Dred Scott was one of those enslaved people. He was born into slavery around 1800. He had several different masters during his life as a slave. One master was a doctor in the army. His name was John Emerson. Because Emerson worked for the army, he moved from place to place. When he first bought Scott, he lived in Missouri. It was a slave state. The army transferred Emerson to the free state of Illinois and to the territory of Wisconsin, where slavery was also prohibited. He took Scott with him.

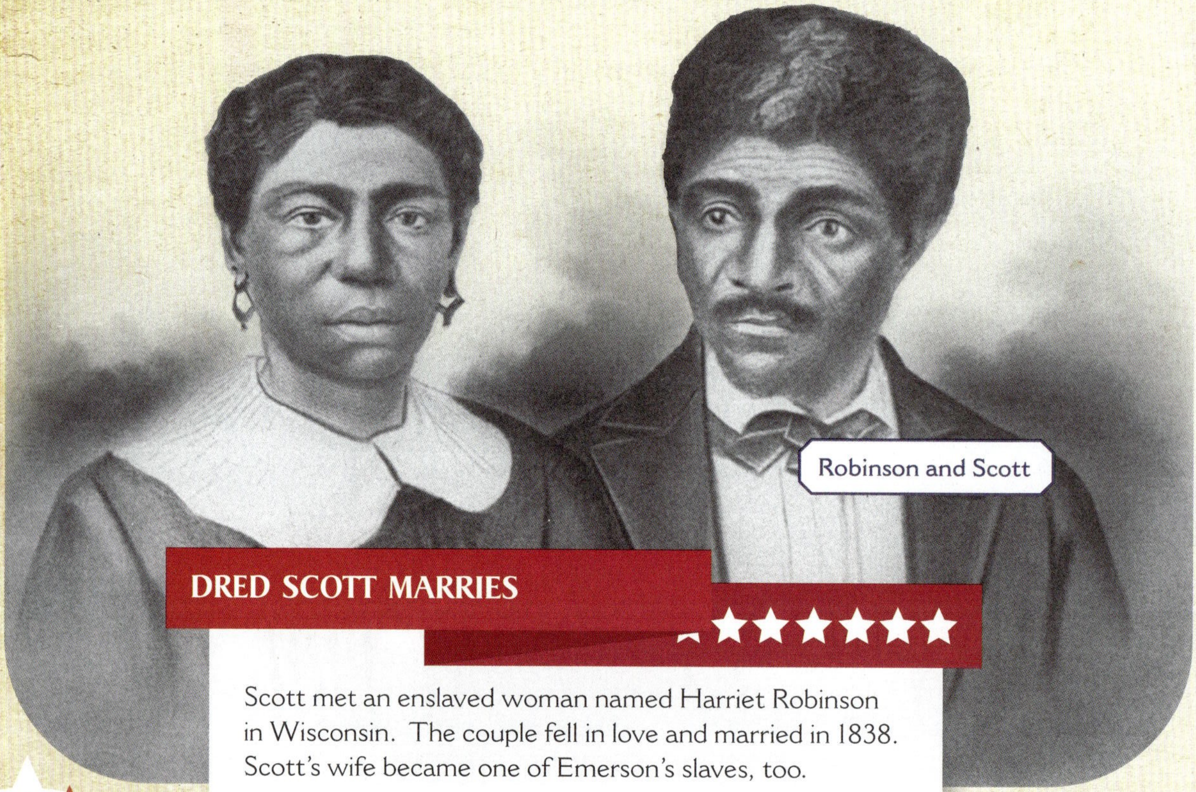

Robinson and Scott

DRED SCOTT MARRIES

Scott met an enslaved woman named Harriet Robinson in Wisconsin. The couple fell in love and married in 1838. Scott's wife became one of Emerson's slaves, too.

Missouri C C U S
#7
Dred Scott plff in Er
vs
John F. A. Sandford
Filed 30th December 1854.
Dismissed
jurisdiction.—
March 6th 1857

Scott became the property of Emerson's wife when Emerson died in 1843. Scott tried to buy his freedom from her for $300, but she refused. So in 1846, Scott decided to sue for his freedom. He said that because he had lived in a free state with his master, he deserved to be free. The case went to the United States' highest court—the U.S. Supreme Court.

This document explains the final decision in the Dred Scott case.

POWER IN PRINT

Harriet Beecher Stowe wrote a story called *Uncle Tom's Cabin*. It was published as a book in 1852. It exposed the horrors of slavery and inspired people to fight to end it.

Harriet Beecher Stowe

The Supreme Court reached a decision in 1857. The Court denied Scott his freedom. The judges said that Scott had no rights because he was a slave. The Court stated that enslaved people were property. They were not U.S. citizens. Therefore, they could not take a case to court. And, the Court reversed the Missouri Compromise. It said that the federal government could not restrict slavery in certain territories.

Supreme Court Chief Justice Roger Brooke Taney (TAW-nee) wrote an opinion for the court. He stated that enslaved people must always obey the law of the state in which they live. Scott had returned to the South to live in a slave state. So, he must obey its laws. Furthermore, Taney wrote that African Americans could never be U.S. citizens.

the courtroom where Dred Scott's trial took place

Chief Justice Taney

Southerners were pleased with the ruling. Northerners were outraged. Some Northern states ignored the Supreme Court's decision. They passed laws that said if slaves were brought to the North, they would be legally free.

The case further divided the country. The North and South could not reach an agreement regarding the issue of slavery. They could not decide whether states had the right to govern themselves. Tensions continued to rise.

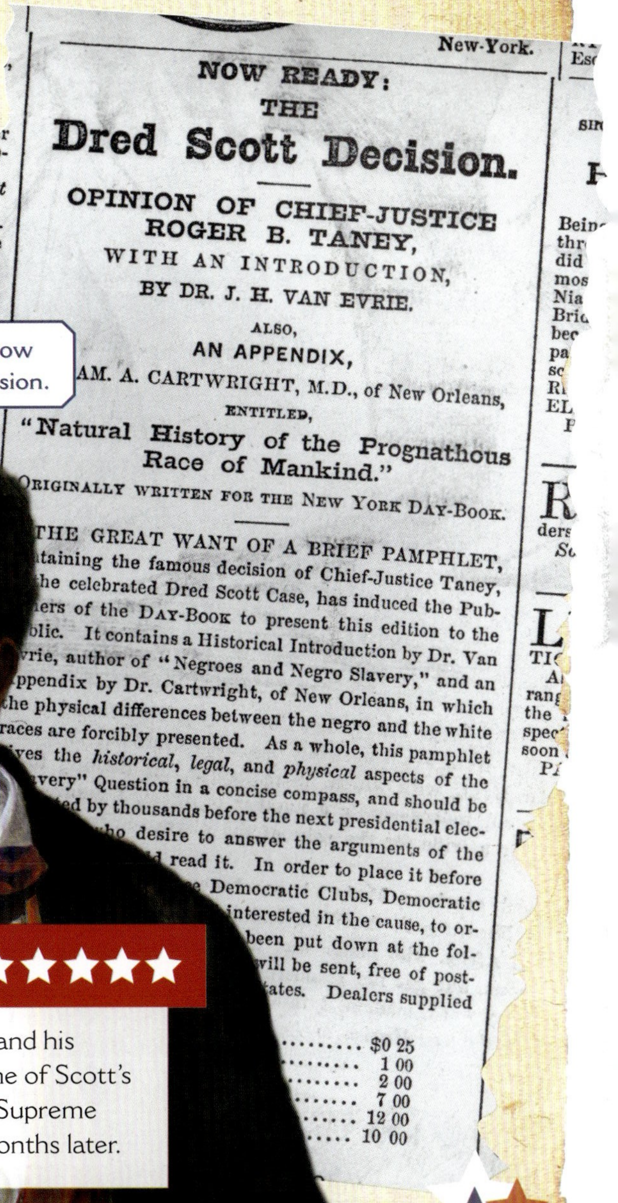

New-York.

NOW READY:

THE

Dred Scott Decision.

OPINION OF CHIEF-JUSTICE ROGER B. TANEY, WITH AN INTRODUCTION, BY DR. J. H. VAN EVRIE.

ALSO,

AN APPENDIX,

[illegible]AM. A. CARTWRIGHT, M.D., of New Orleans,

ENTITLED,

"Natural History of the Prognathous Race of Mankind."

[O]RIGINALLY WRITTEN FOR THE NEW YORK DAY-BOOK.

[T]HE GREAT WANT OF A BRIEF PAMPHLET, [con]taining the famous decision of Chief-Justice Taney, [in t]he celebrated Dred Scott Case, has induced the Pub[lish]ers of the DAY-BOOK to present this edition to the [pu]blic. It contains a Historical Introduction by Dr. Van [Ev]rie, author of "Negroes and Negro Slavery," and an [A]ppendix by Dr. Cartwright, of New Orleans, in which the physical differences between the negro and the white races are forcibly presented. As a whole, this pamphlet [gi]ves the *historical*, *legal*, and *physical* aspects of the ["Sla]very" Question in a concise compass, and should be [rea]d by thousands before the next presidential elec[tion, w]ho desire to answer the arguments of the [illegible] read it. In order to place it before [illegible] Democratic Clubs, Democratic [illegible] interested in the cause, to or[illegible] been put down at the fol[illegible] will be sent, free of post[age illegible]tates. Dealers supplied

....	$0 25
....	1 00
....	2 00
....	7 00
....	12 00
....	10 00

This newspaper ad tells people how they can order a copy of the decision.

FREE AT LAST

Dred Scott got his freedom in the end. He and his family got transferred back to the sons of one of Scott's previous owners. They freed him after the Supreme Court's decision. Sadly, Scott died a few months later.

Raid and Revolt

John Brown was born in 1800. He grew up in the North. He and his family were antislavery. They believed it was a **sin** against God. By 1859, Brown was working hard to abolish slavery. He felt he was doing God's work. He gave speeches against slavery and helped enslaved people escape to freedom in the North. But he felt that this was not enough. Things were moving too slowly. So, Brown devised a plan. He would lead a **revolt**.

Brown chose Harpers Ferry, Virginia, as the site of his revolt. There was a federal **armory** there. He wanted to raid the armory and steal its guns. He planned to give these guns to enslaved people in the area. Then, he would lead them in a revolt against their owners. It was an extremely dangerous plan. Attacking a federal armory was an act of **treason**. But Brown was determined.

NOT THE FIRST TIME

In an attempt to drive **abolitionists** out of Bleeding Kansas, a proslavery group attacked an office. Brown and his sons planned their own assault. They found and killed five of the men they believed were associated with the attack.

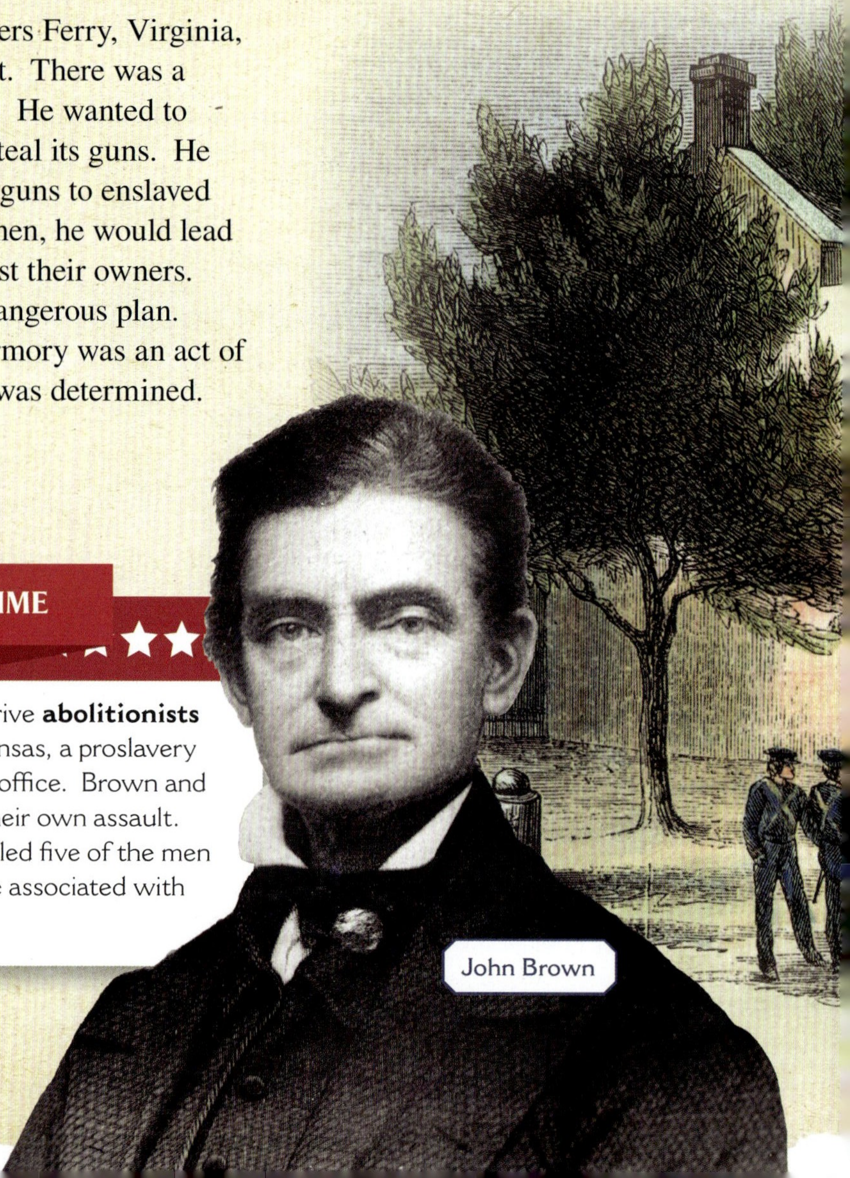

John Brown

Frederick Douglass

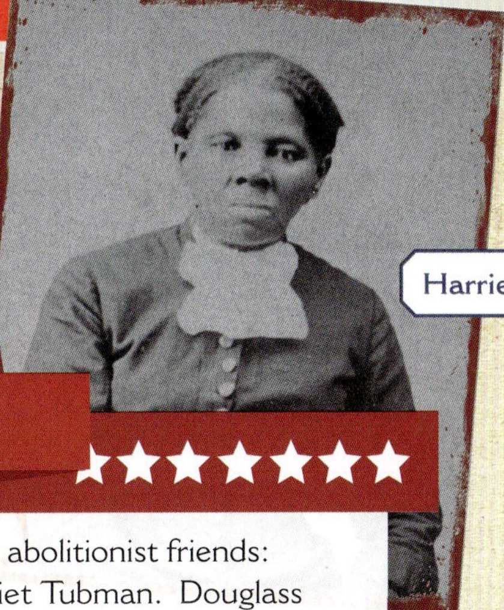

Harriet Tubman

FAMOUS FRIENDS

John Brown had two famous abolitionist friends: Frederick Douglass and Harriet Tubman. Douglass warned Brown not to proceed with his plan. Tubman, on the other hand, supported Brown. She wanted to be a part of the raid. But, she became ill and was unable to participate.

Brown's raid on the armory at Harpers Ferry

Brown's plan was put into action in October of 1859. He traveled to Harpers Ferry with a group of 21 men. Most were white, including two of Brown's sons. The first thing the men did was capture the federal armory. They took weapons. They used them to round up the town's leaders and hold them **hostage**.

Brown and his men expected local enslaved people to join them in the attack. They hoped the revolt would grow even bigger as they traveled to other parts of the country. But, the enslaved people in the area were not prepared to fight. They did not come forward. Instead, the town's **militia** (mi-LISH-uh) went on the offensive. They fought back, wounding and killing many of Brown's men.

In the end, Brown surrendered. He was charged with treason, murder, and slave **insurrection**. He was sentenced to hang. Brown's revolt did not succeed. Yet, his actions had a larger impact. Southerners grew fearful of violent slave revolts. Northerners decided that they had to take action. Both sides prepared for war.

John Brown holds his dying son at Harpers Ferry.

REACTION TO THE RAID

Some people called Brown a hero. Others called him a terrorist and viewed him as a criminal who had broken the law and used violence to try and achieve his goal.

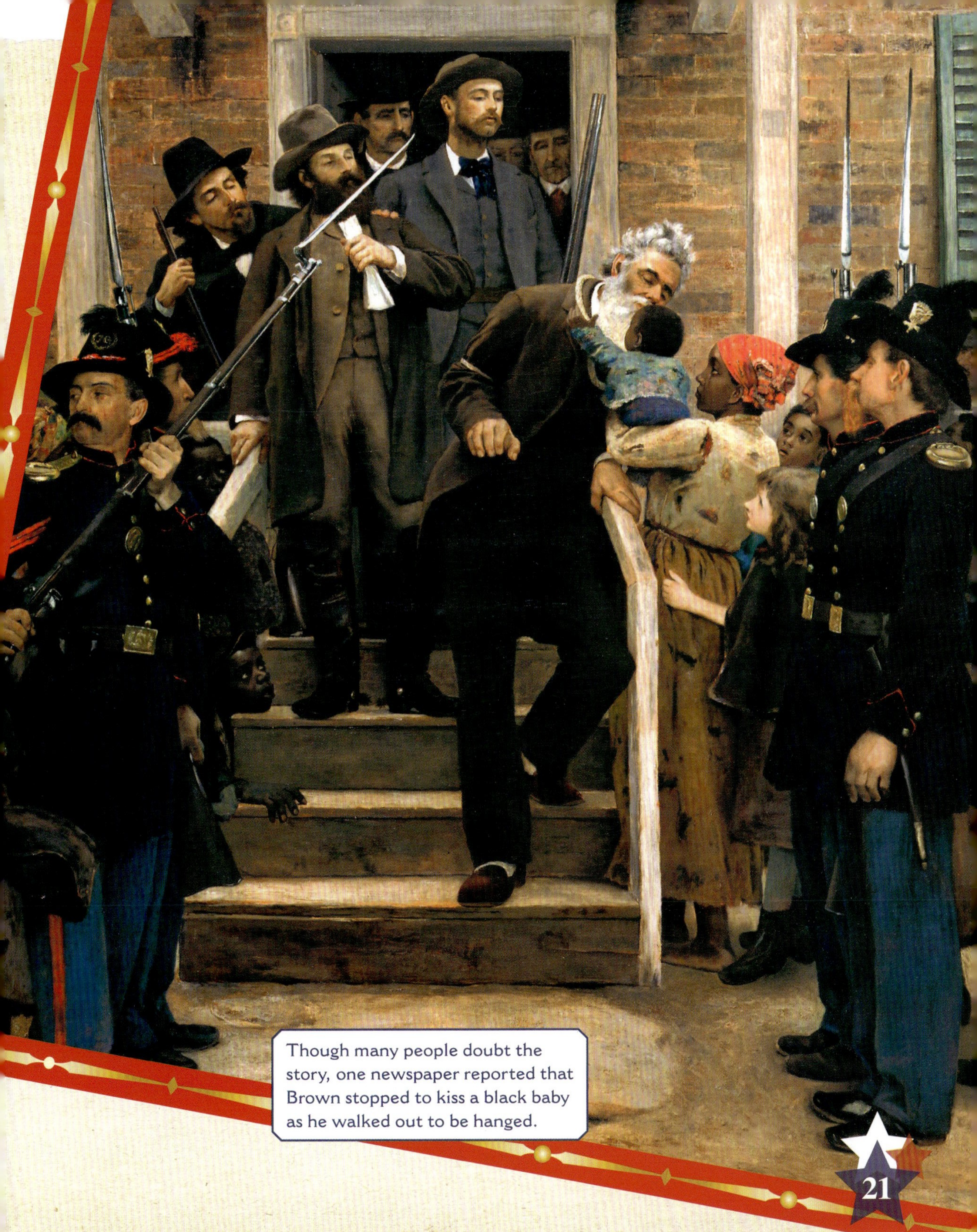

Though many people doubt the story, one newspaper reported that Brown stopped to kiss a black baby as he walked out to be hanged.

Deepening the Divide

In 1858, there was an open seat in the Senate. Stephen A. Douglas was a Democrat who already held a seat. Abraham Lincoln was a Republican. He decided to run against Douglas. The winner would represent the state of Illinois in Congress.

The men held seven debates. These were known as the Lincoln-Douglas debates. Lincoln argued that slavery was morally wrong. Douglas claimed that equal rights were for white men only. Their words traveled by **telegraph** and by train. The entire country heard their speeches. People took sides. The nation grew more divided. In the end, Douglas won the seat.

LEADING THE CONFEDERACY

Before Lincoln even took office, South Carolina, Mississippi, Florida, Alabama, Georgia, Louisiana, and Texas all **seceded** from the Union. They called themselves the Confederate States of America. They were later joined by Arkansas, North Carolina, Tennessee, and Virginia.

1860 campaign banner for Lincoln

In 1860, Lincoln and Douglas faced off once more—but this time it was for the presidency. The men had different ideas about how to run the country. Lincoln did not want the nation to stay divided. He wanted to slowly end slavery. Douglas believed the country should continue as it was. He thought it should stay divided into free and slave states.

Lincoln did not have any support from Southerners. His name was not even on ballots in the South. Yet, he won. He became the next president. Leaders of Southern states were outraged. They started to secede from the Union. They formed their own government.

This 1860 political cartoon shows Lincoln and Douglas fighting for the presidency.

Lincoln is sworn in as the 16th president of the United States.

Lincoln took office in March of 1861. He knew he had a big and complicated task ahead of him. The country was at a breaking point. Many questions needed to be answered. Would the Union dissolve now that Southern states had left it? Would there be peace? Would there be war?

Lincoln's first speech as president was hopeful. He called for peace between the North and the South. "We are not enemies, but friends," he said. "Though passion may have strained, it must not break our bonds of affection."

Yet, Lincoln also made it clear in that same speech that he would not tolerate secession. The Union would fight to keep the country united as one. He said it was up to the South to keep the peace. "In your hands, my dissatisfied fellow-countrymen, and not in mine, is the momentous issue of civil war," he said. However, the Confederate states were ready and willing to fight.

THE SECESSION CRISIS

James Buchanan (byoo-KAH-nehn) was president before Lincoln. He was supposed to handle the secession crisis. But, he did not address the issue. As he left office, war was brewing.

Country in Crisis

In 1861, the United States was a country in crisis. It was split in two by differing opinions. It was now North versus South. Neither side could agree on slavery. Nor could they agree on states' rights. But, they both agreed it was time for war.

Would slavery continue? Would states keep their rights? Could the country unite once more? Only the Civil War would answer these questions and settle the dispute. On April 12, 1861, the first shots were fired. The war had begun. It took four long and bloody years to come to an end.

Charleston residents watch the first battle of the Civil War at Fort Sumter.

Soldiers defend Fort Sumter.

The Civil War is arguably the most violent encounter on U.S. soil. It divided the nation. In some cases, family members fought against one another. The losses to both sides were terrible. But, in the end, enslaved people were made free. States' rights vs. federal rights are still debated. Some people say the Civil War and what caused it are still in effect today.

WITNESS TO HISTORY

Dred Scott's wife, Harriet, was born into slavery around 1815. After gaining her freedom in 1857, she worked for pay and owned her own home. She lived to see the end of slavery in the United States.

Rap It!

Think about the events leading up to the Civil War. What caused the country to split apart? Write a rap that describes the causes of the Civil War. Include important topics, such as slavery and the raid at Harpers Ferry. Discuss key players such as Dred Scott and Abraham Lincoln. Explain the different views the North and the South held. Then, gather your friends and family and perform your rap.

FRANK LESLIE'S
ILLUSTRATED
NEWSPAPER
NEW YORK, SATURDAY, JUNE 27, 1857.
No. 82.—VOL. IV.]
VISIT TO DRED SCOTT—HIS FAMILY—INCIDENTS OF HIS LIFE—DECISION OF THE SUPREME COURT.

MAP OF THE
AREAS OF SECESSION
Scale of Miles
0 50 100 200 300 400
GULF OF MEXICO
TEXAS
LOUISIANA
MISSISSIPPI
ALABAMA
GEORGIA
FLORIDA
SOUTH CAROLINA
NORTH CAROLINA
TENNESSEE
ARKANSAS
INDIAN TERRITORY
KENTUCKY
MISSOURI
KANSAS
NEBRASKA
IOWA
ILLINOIS
INDIANA
OHIO
WEST VIRGINIA
VIRGINIA

Glossary

abolish—to officially end or stop something

abolitionists—people who were against slavery and worked to end it

armory—a place where weapons are kept

compromise—to give up something you want in order to reach an agreement

controversial—something which is disagreed upon for a long time

debates—discussions between people who have differing opinions

doctrine—a statement of government policy

economy—the system of buying and selling goods and services

federal—relating to the main government of the United States

hostage—a person who is held against his or her will until certain things are done; against one's will

insurrection—a violent attempt to take control

militia—regular citizens trained in military combat and willing to fight and defend their country

revolt—to fight in a violent way against a leader or government

seceded—formally separated from a nation or state

sin—an action that is thought to be wrong by moral or religious standards

sued—brought a lawsuit against someone

telegraph—an old-fashioned system of sending messages over long distances by using wires and electrical signals

treason—the crime of betraying one's own country by waging war against it

Union—term used to describe the United States of America; also the name given to the Northern army during the Civil War

Index

Your Turn!

CAUTION!!

COLORED PEOPLE

OF BOSTON, ONE & ALL,

You are hereby respectfully CAUTIONED and advised, to avoid conversing with the

Watchmen and Police Officers of Boston,

For since the recent ORDER OF THE MAYOR & ALDERMEN, they are empowered to act as

KIDNAPPERS

AND

Slave Catchers,

And they have already been actually employed in KIDNAPPING, CATCHING, AND KEEPING SLAVES. Therefore, if you value your LIBERTY, and the *Welfare of the Fugitives* among you, *Shun* them in every possible manner, as so many *HOUNDS* on the track of the most unfortunate of your race.

Keep a Sharp Look Out for KIDNAPPERS, and have TOP EYE open.

APRIL 24, 1851.

Warning Poster

This poster from 1851 is a warning to African Americans in Boston about slave catchers. It was written shortly after the Fugitive Slave Act was revised. How does the language used in the poster show the writer's feelings about the law? How does it show the division in the United States at that time? Write a brief paragraph to answer these questions.